John Henry King

THREE HUNDRED DAYS IN A YANKEE PRISON

Reminiscences of Camp Chase, Ohio

by

John Henry King

THE CONFEDERATE
REPRINT COMPANY

☆ ☆ ☆ ☆

WWW.CONFEDERATEREPRINT.COM

Three Hundred Days in a Yankee Prison
Reminiscences of Camp Chase, Ohio
by John Henry King

Originally Published in 1904
by James P. Daves
Atlanta, Georgia

The Confederate Reprint Company
Post Office Box 2027
Toccoa, Georgia 30577
www.confederatereprint.com

Cover and Interior Design by
Magnolia Graphic Design
www.magnoliagraphicdesign.com

ISBN-13: 978-0692737187
ISBN-10: 0692737189

PREFACE

☆ ☆ ☆ ☆

Very much has been written and much more embodied in the partial reports and *ex parte* investigations of the so-called "Horrors of Andersonville" and the "inhuman treatment" of the prisoners of the Federal armies by the prison officials, and the agents of the Confederate State's War Department. These publications have emanated from the press of Northern publishers and have been inspired by a spirit of enmity which is evidently partisan and extremely vindictive. Doubtless, much that has been thus detailed of the privations and sufferings of the prisoners captured by our Confederate armies and sent for security to prison camps, is true. From the very nature of the imprisonment, prison life, at best, is one of privation. "War is hell on earth" said General Sherman when attempting to justify the enormity of acts perpetrated by his troops on the defenseless women and children of Georgia during his march to the sea. If there be any doubt of the truth of Sherman's declaration, he certainly made the proof of it conclusive as he rode at the head of an army that brought the terrors of Hell to the defenseless people of Georgia and the Carolinas, when his legions went plundering, murdering, and like savages, pillaging and then burning the homes of unresisting non-combatants. The rules and usages of civilized warfare require that all non-combatants should be immune from capture and that their rights of property should be respected, and furthermore, that combatants should be held when captured as prisoners until properly exchanged; and, while under restraint as prisoners, that they should receive the same rations of food as were issued soldiers of the line, being treated, not as criminals, but as soldiers worthy of the respect and consideration of a chivalrous enemy. Such was the uniform practice in the early period of our Civil War, especially with the regularly organized opposing armies, and so it continued to be with these armies until the end of the war.

It was only with these irregular bands of "Bush Whackers," Guerrillas, and Rangers that prisoners, captured in battle, were badly treated.

At an early date in the war a cartel of exchange of prisoners captured in battle was agreed upon between the Federal and Confederate governments. Under this cartel there was no unnecessary delay in the exchange, but as the war progressed the cartel was modified, suspended or disregarded by the Federal war office to suit the expediency of a brutal war minister, Mr. Stanton, who, to secure the triumph of the partisan cause, violated every law of civilized warfare and with the zeal of a fanatic, inaugurated a savage rule of extermination.

It was discovered by the savage exponent of the radical war party at the North, that as soon as a Confederate soldier was exchanged for one of their hirelings, the Confederate at once took his place in the ranks of the patriot army, willing and ready to devote his life in the defence of the cause he believed to be just, and of a people he knew to be shamefully outraged. On the contrary, the hireling, the pauper recruit, from some one of the European States, would in the majority of instances, under some subterfuge, sneak to the rear and wait the contingency of a pension for meritorious service. At once the zealous Secretary of War found some pretext for suspending the cartel of exchange of prisoners, and for inaugurating a system of slow and certain death at the Federal prisons that will make the history of Camp Chase, Johnson's Island, Fort Delaware, and other prison pens in the frozen North, a monumental record of Stanton's brutality and the mean, vindictive spirit of his partisans.

There was, and there yet remains, an undeniable excuse for the Confederate treatment of the prisoners confined at Libby, Belle Isle and elsewhere. Their want of abundant food so much com-plained of, came from the same cause that made the empty haversacks of our own soldiers in the field. Compare these rations issued to the Confederate army with the rations regularly issued to the prisoners at Andersonville, and who among the half-starved patriots of the Confederate army would not have gladly exchanged with them?

Finding it impossible to defeat the Confederate army in an open, manly contest on the battlefield, even with the odds of three and four to one, the plan of starving these invincible battalions was resorted to, even though in starving them they were rendering it impossible to furnish their own prisoners with a soldier's rations.

An order issued to make desolate the Valley of Virginia (how cowardly!), Sheridan, with his torch in one hand and their savage order near his brutal heart, moved an army of marauders over this fertile region, the granary of the South. His terrible mission ended, with remorseless exultation he informed his master, "I have made the valley so desolate that a crow to live will have to carry army rations on his back as he flies over these hills and valleys." He might have added: "And I have left in the bleak winds of winter more than one thousand women and children without a sheltering home or a crumb of bread."

While Sheridan was thus trying to starve the army of General Lee, he was destroying the food that would have gone in part to the prisoners at Andersonville.

It is safe to say that the thousands of cattle and hogs and the countless bushels of wheat, corn and potatoes burned and wasted by Sherman's army on its barbarous march through Georgia, would have fed the Andersonville prisoners for months. At Oconee, on the Central Railway of Georgia, Howard's corps burned two trains of cars loaded with corn meal, flour and bacon, on the way to feed the Andersonville prisoners. When informed by the conductor of the train of this fact, he was answered by Howard's commissary that he did not believe him and ordered the conductor under guard as a prisoner and forthwith set fire to his cars. When asked why he did not take the flour and bacon for the use of his army, he answered, "We have more now than we can haul; our men have been feeding on chickens, turkeys, milk and honey ever since we left Atlanta."

Again when prisoners had accumulated in such large numbers at our prisons to render it impossible to furnish them with other than the plainest food; when, owing to the blockade of our ports, and from the further fact that quinine and other medicines had been declared "contraband of war" by the Federal authorities, every possible effort was made by the Confederate Secretary of War to secure a general exchange of prisoners. A frank statement of the conditions which rendered it impossible to give to the prisoners other than the service they were receiving, was made as an appeal for humanity's sake; made to secure their release by resuming the cartel for a general exchange of all the prisoners held on both sides. This was refused. Had this exchange been made it would have added several thousand good recruits to the Confederate armies and, man for man, would have still left a large surplus of Federal prisoners in the Confederate camps of detention.

Our Confederate Secretary of War, through his commissioner, Col. Ould, then offered to receive quinine and other much-needed medicine and any commissary supplies that might be sent to the Federal prisoners for their exclusive use. This offer was also refused by the Federal Secretary of War. Thus it is a matter of historical fact that the real cause of any suffering among the prisoners held either at Andersonville or elsewhere in the South, was the refusal of the Federal Government to carry out in good faith the human and equitable cartel of exchange agreed upon in the early period of the war, and to recognize and conform to the usages of war between civilized and enlightened nations.

As to the climate and its effect upon the constitutions of the unacclimated persons, the Confederate government was in no wise responsible. Our Secretary of War was not the Lord of the winds nor the Prince of the air. He could not rule the rays of the sun or the dews of the night. All he could do, and that was done, was to select the healthiest places in the South, where the prisoners could be held secure and provide them with such rations and comforts as were issued to our soldiers in the field.

How was it with our prisoners in the pens and camps in the bleak regions of the North? There could be no possible excuse for starving them, since they were in a land of abundance. No armies had desolated their teeming grain fields; no torches had burned their mills or destroyed their immense store-houses of food. The poor prisoner could look wistfully out from his cheerless pen upon all of this teeming abundance only to suffer the pangs of "Tantalus" while slowly starving to death. There was food almost in his grasp. However, we give the detail of this suffering and of "man's inhumanity to man" in the succeeding pages.

From the standpoint of a private soldier in the Confederate army the author presents a truthful account of his capture, imprisonment, and sufferings in a Federal prison. Hundreds, who like himself, endured these pangs will find in these pages experiences that they have realized and from which, like him, they have only escaped with life, through the intervention of a divine Providence. Let those who still harp on the "cruelties of Andersonville," read the other side of this wretched story and then, if they are honest, the wonder will be that they have not sooner discovered the "beam" in their own eyes.

Close-up of the memorial boulder at Camp Chase Confederate Cemetery.

CHAPTER ONE

☆ ☆ ☆ ☆

Leaving Home – Tocsin of War In the Ranks – Cumberland Gap – Vicksburg – Wounded and Captured

If you were living in Georgia, gentle reader, in the early months of the year of Grace, 1862, you can recall the martial spirit that reigned supreme among our citizens, old and young, male and female.

The tocsin of war had called into the ranks of regiments and battalions, the arms-bearing men of our once peaceful and prosperous State. From the blood-stained field of Manassas, in Virginia, over their beautiful valleys and from the summits of our grand mountains, from the prairies of Texas and the fruitful plains of Mississippi, the roll of the drum and the bugle's shrill blast echoed and re-echoed the call to arms.

To be patriotic then, was but to obey the impulse of a nature formed amid the surroundings and taught in the school of a proud and chivalrous people. To fail in answering this clarion note from those whom we had long trusted and admired as our leaders, was to meet a coward's rebuke from father, mother, sister, sweetheart and friend.

I was quite young, not yet within several years of my majority. Never of an impulsive disposition, I had time for reflection before offering my life in a service I knew to be attended with many hazards and exposures, to which I was in no manner accustomed. Three elder brothers had months before joined their neighbors in the rank of our patriot army, and had from their experiences sent back to a venerable father details of privations incident to a soldier's life in front of the enemy on the plains and among the mountains of Virginia.

These reports, which I knew were not exaggerated, could not encourage the hope that I would escape a soldier's rough life on the march, in the bivouac, in the camp, or the dangers of the battlefield.

Of my brothers, one was killed in battle, another died of disease contracted in the army, and the third severely wounded while following the colors of his regiment.

My father, conservative in thought and deliberate in action, had opposed the secession of Georgia from the Federal union, which he believed, with Alexander Stephens, Herschell V. Johnson, Benjamin Hill and other Southern statesmen, to be unwise and fraught only with dire consequences; yet when a majority of his fellow-citizens had, through their representatives in convention assembled, taken the hazardous step, one his judgment could not approve, he stood firmly by their action and offered a sacrifice of life and fortune on the altar of patriotism. With him it was, "My mother, right or wrong, my mother!"

In my childhood's young morning, death had taken to an angelic home the light and the love of his life. No mother was at the hearthstone of our homestead to cheer with her presence our family gathering, to bless with her love the children, to whom she had left as a legacy her womanly virtues. This bereavement seemed to draw closer to my father those who were remaining pledges of a holy love. One can only know in the profound depths of its sacredness, who has experienced the reciprocal affections of congenial natures. Under such circumstances it would be but natural to suppose that a man of my father's temperament would desire to keep near to his presence the sons who were given as the heritage of a good man by the Author of his being. Yet he did not hesitate to make an offering of these, although we well knew that the sacrifice caused him hours of grief and gloomy forebodings of evil. By no word or act did he discourage my enlistment in the service of Georgia or the Confederacy. His was not a demonstrative disposition, but in the quiet expressions which grief gave to his countenance, could be plainly read the emotions of his manly heart.

When the hour of departure came, and I was ready to leave a happy childhood home, standing on its threshold, he bade me good-bye, with the injunction: "Do your duty, my son, and never let me hear that you have been guilty of cowardice or a dishonorable act."

The regiment to which my company was attached was organized at "Big Shanty," now known as "Kennesaw," on the Western and Atlantic Railway, and there I began my soldier's career and formed the comradeship of the camp and the march. The regiment numbered in the order of enlistment as the 10th Georgia Infantry and was under the command of Col. Abda Johnson, my company being designated by the letter "H." From "Big Shanty" our regiment was ordered to Camp Van Dorn, near Knoxville, Tennessee, where we remained several months drilling and preparing for the field of action. When considered ready for duty, the regiment was ordered to Powell's Valley, near Cumberland Gap, where we found ourselves to be the pioneer troops in this, an enemy's country. Notwithstanding, we were yet in Tennessee, one of the Southern sisterhood of States, we soon discovered that we were among a people who were the bitter and uncompromising enemies of the Confederate cause; we were, in fact, among the mountaineers of East Tennessee, an ignorant, prejudiced people, who were under the control and absolutely dominated by the Brownlow, Johnson, Maynard school of radical republicanism. These people had been led to believe by their politicians that the cause of the Confederacy was an effort of the slaveholder to establish an oligarchy, in which the planters of the cotton and rice producing States would install for all time an aristocracy on the ruins of democratic institutions. They had made a demigod of Brownlow, whose radical republican doctrines were of the extremest socialism, and were blindly following his lead. From the earliest period of our Colonial history these exponents of extreme democratic social doctrines had been a source of annoyance and of revolutionary sedition. Coming from the lowest walks of life in England, they became in America the "camp-followers" of the gentry, who under grants from the Crown were planting English civilization on the American continent. Driven from the settlements near the Atlantic coast, these social anarchists of the seventeenth century found refuge in the mountains of western North Carolina and East Tennessee, and there, for many generations their descendants have continued to live, spreading out along the range of the Blue Ridge, the Cumberland and Allegheny mountains north and south, adhering always and naturally to an antipathy for all that is refined, courtly or chivalrous. To live in a squalid hut of one room, in which a large family would dwell, year after year, with no distinction between sexes, and which was bare of all ornament, unless you would consider the cheap lithograph of a favorite Jack, or of a prancing stallion an ornament, and which invited the winds of winter and the bugs of summer to freely enter; to loiter among the great forest with a long squirrel rifle or lounge about some blacksmith shop or grocery, adding to the gossip and chit-chat of empty minds under the inspiration of corn whiskey; to praise Parson Brownlow, then to poison a spring-house, or to lay a blind from which to kill a Confederate soldier, made the *"ultima thule"* of a mountaineer's ambition in the wilds of East Tennessee in 1862. They appeared not only to condemn all that had the semblance of decency, but in reality boasted of their freedom from everything that had even the appearance of respectability. In all of which they were but illustrating the characteristics of their ancestors who had come from the slums, the prison cells, the stocks and whipping-posts of London and other English cities near two centuries gone by. To distinguish this class from the more respected citizens our Confederate soldiers gave them the name of "Hogbacks." It was very natural that they should become the "bushwhackers," who at a safe distance behind some rocky cliff, would often fire upon our passing troops or expose to view in some cool spring-house a jug or pan of poisoned milk.

The small force comprising the Confederate army, commanded by General Stevenson, occupied the valley southeast of the Cumberland mountains, within easy marching distance of Cumberland Gap, then occupied by a Federal garrison under the command of the Union general Morgan. So far we were only employed watching the movements of our enemy, whose pickets would occasionally exchange shots with those of us who, on like duty, were at the extreme front of our small army. This service was so free from excitement that as the days and weeks passed by without a battle to relieve its monotony, we began to think the war would be ended before we had shared in the glory of a single victory. We had but to wait until our army was reinforced sufficiently for the hazard, and then for the first time I was to feel that peculiar thrill known to all gallant soldiers as the glamour of battle. It was in the early fall of 1862 that the rattle of drums and the bugle's shrill blast assured us that the hour had come and now really we were to receive a soldier's baptism in the smoke and carnage of the battlefield. Judged from later experiences, and when compared with many other battles that in subsequent years followed it, this combat at Tazwell dwindles into not much more than a first-class skirmish. However, it was my initial experience, the first time that in martial array I had witnessed hostile armies in the grapple of deadly conflict, and, of course, for weeks after formed the fruitful theme of many letters descriptive of personal prowess and gallant achievements. Some one of his many biographers relates that when Arthur Wellesley, afterwards the great Duke of Wellington, was on his first battlefield as a young lieutenant in the British army, he was noticed by a burly old veteran to evidence considerable nervous excitement. Approaching the young lieutenant, his old sergeant exclaimed: "What! Wellesley, are you going to be a coward in this your maiden fight?" To which the lieutenant promptly replied: "Sir, if you felt half as bad as I do now, you would leave the battlefield." One was held to his post by the influence of mere physical courage, such as a bulldog evidences, while the other was there and to remain under the stimulus of a moral force, the highest possible expression of human courage. If I could have been relieved of all sense of duty and have reasoned at all from the standpoint of a mere animal, when rifle balls were whistling about my head and shells exploding in our ranks, I would certainly have sought some safer place, but, thank God, I was not made of such gross material. The parting injunction of my father was in my memory, the cause of my country nearer to my soul than the safety of my person. Like all new recruits I could not but feel a peculiar trepidation, but I was there to do my duty, even if it was to meet death.

The result of the battle of Tazwell was a victory for our army, one of several that made the year 1862 a splendid chapter in the glorious history of the Confederate armies. The mongrel army of "bushwhackers," "hogbacks" and their Federal soldiers retreated to Cumberland Gap, where they were closely besieged, all communication with Kentucky being cut off by the advance of General Kirby Smith through Big Creek Gap. General Morgan found himself completely checkmated. In his front was our army, in his rear the army of General Kirby Smith, on his right flank, at Big Creek, Ga., a vigilant force under Col. H. D. Capers, and on his left a division under the command of General Humphrey Marshall. Col. Capers by a rapid march surprised the Federal garrison at Huntsville, Tennessee, and destroyed a large depot of quartermaster and commissary supplies, the only base from which General Morgan could furnish his troops with clothing or provisions. Owing to carelessness on the part of General Marshall's advanced brigade, a road or the ridge of the mountain leading into southwestern Virginia was unguarded, and by this Morgan made his escape, drawing off his garrison at night and evacuating the gap, leaving his heavy artillery and camp equipage as a trophy for General Stevenson. As soon as it was ascertained that the Federal army had escaped capture, our division was at once ordered to join General Smith in Kentucky, and took up the line of march to the "dark and bloody ground," famous the world over for its fine horses, lovely women and Bourbon whiskey.

It is not my purpose in this memoir to give in detail a history of the campaign of General Bragg in Kentucky or of the administration of his department in subsequent movements on the chess board of war. Others more competent have done this, and while General Bragg undoubtedly deserves the severest criticisms which his repeated failures and bad generalship fully merit, no possible reflection can be made on the courage and the gallantry of the rank and file of his superb army. The corps under General Smith, which formed the right of General Bragg's army of invasion, after a brilliant victory at Richmond, Kentucky, was in undisputed possession of eastern and much of the Blue Grass region of this fertile and beautiful country. On all hands we saw the evidences of abounding thrift and were met by demonstrations of approval from hundreds whose fathers, sons and brothers had either joined our army or were in sympathy with our cause. General Smith had established his headquarters at Lexington and had pushed his advanced brigades under General Neath to the Ohio river, opposite Cincinnati, while with the main army General Bragg occupied the center of the State from Bowling Green to Frankfort.

Our troops, elated with success, were in the highest spirits, well equipped and abundantly supplied from the apparently inexhaustible store-houses of a section that had so far escaped the ravages of contending armies. We began to feel confident of a permanent lodgement in this "land of milk and honey," when out from Louisville General Buell marched his strongly re-enforced army and forced General Bragg to battle before he could concentrate his widely separated divisions. The bloody battle of Perryville ensued, fought almost exclusively by the Army of Mississippi, on our side, commanded by Generals Polk and Hardee. It is safe to say that if General Bragg had kept his army corps within easy supporting distance, Perryville, instead of being a drawn battle, would have proved a splendid triumph for our arms, and would have brought thousands of undecided Kentuckians to the active support of our cause. Had Stonewall Jackson been in command of our superb army the result would have been far different. But I desist. There was, unhappily for the cause of Dixie, only one Stonewall Jackson, whose genius, courage and energy could not be, or certainly was not, imparted to the favorites of President Davis. After Perryville, began the retreat of our army back to Tennessee through Cumberland Gap. If we had entered Kentucky with spirits elated by success, we returned to our camping ground of the summer and fall, dispirited, weary, half-famished and with no great admiration for our commanding general. Only a brief rest in Powell's Valley and then we marched to Lenoirs on the East Tennessee, Virginia and Georgia Railroad, where we were ordered into camp to recuperate the wasted energies of an unsuccessful campaign. General Bragg could not exclaim with Caesar, "*Veni, vidi, vici,*" but he could say that he was a general, who, having marched up a hill, marched down again.

After a rest of two or three weeks at Lenoirs, began one of the longest and most trying marches of my soldier's experiences. Our orders took us to Murfreesboro, Tennessee, over two hundred miles distant, and through the roughest and most uninviting country. It was indeed with us a long, toilsome climb up hill, to be followed by a stumbling slide down hill, until finally we reached our destination foot-sore, weary and worn, and went into camp on Stone River, where soon was to be fought one of the bloodiest and most undecisive battles of the war. Here we remained a few days, when orders came to cook rations and prepare for another long march to reinforce our army at Vicksburg, Mississippi.

Fortunately, we were on a line of railway and, while we escaped the bloody ordeal of Stone River and Murfreesboro and the rough tramp of our march from Lenoirs, our destination was into the vortex of battle and to a besieged garrison whose sufferings no pen can fully describe. On the 28th and 29th of December we were in line of battle, opposing a large force of the enemy at Chickasaw Bayou, Mississippi, above Vicksburg. Here a hotly contested battle raged in all the fury of war, lasting through many hours of desperate struggling until the enemy gave way and retreated to the Mississippi River under the shelter of his gunboats. This was my introduction to the army defending Vicksburg, where I was destined to remain and to endure the privations of a besieged garrison for many long months. Finding it impossible to capture the city or to force its evacuation by an approach from the north on the eastern side of the river, this bloody repulse at Chickasaw Bayou determined General Grant to cross his army to the west bank and make an effort to change the channel of the great "Father of Waters" by digging a canal across the loop made by the river in front of Vicksburg. Through this canal he hoped to convey his army supplies, fully protected from the fire of our well-constructed and well-manned batteries, while he was preparing to move upon Vicksburg from the east and south. In this General Grant was disappointed. The old river refused to obey his mandate and remained as silent in response to his command as did the ocean to the order of King Canute.

Failing in this engineering undertaking the desperate enterprise of running the fire of our batteries with his transports was resorted to, under cover of a terrific bombardment of the city by a mortar fleet stationed in the channel of the river. The water batteries, indeed all the defensive works of Vicksburg, were well-constructed by engineers of great skill and experience and our heavy guns, especially in the river batteries, served by cool and well-trained gunners, soon became the terror of the Federal fleet. To the uninitiated infantry soldier who had become in a measure indifferent to the staccato notes of rifle balls there was an appalling sensation produced by the constantly descending mortar shells whose peculiar hissing sound as they descended in graceful curves, was followed by an explosion that was really more demoralizing to the nerves than dangerous to the body. It was impossible to make more than a conjecture as to where these shells would fall and as they came constantly day and night, if you were in range of the mortars from which they were thrown, an ever present apprehension of danger gave, at least to me, an ever present sense of insecurity.

The devoted citizens were forced to leave their dwellings, whose wrecked walls and ruined lawns and gardens were on every street the evidences of the destructive genius of ruthless war. In improvised "dugouts" and in artificial caves whole families would take refuge from the pitiless shells. Some of these were quite extensive and made as secure as the "bomb-proof" of a fort. Subterranean passageways would lead to rooms of considerable dimensions, fitted up with some of the comforts and conveniences of a home. It was really inspiring to witness the cheerful submission of the gallant old men and their noblest of kinswomen to all of these privations. No murmuring complaint did I hear nor the sigh of a tearful regret. Patriotism never made a more willing sacrifice than the good people of Vicksburg offered. at the altar of their country's cause.

On the night of the 16th of April the enemy's fleet made an attempt to pass our batteries. Seven of his gunboats and transports succeeded, one being burned, another sunk, and the remainder forced to put back. At no time during my service did I witness a greater display of the terrific grandeur of war than upon this ever memorable occasion. No pyrotechnic exhibition, however elaborate, could excel or approximate the scene, and no din of battle ever made its infernal echoes roll in louder tones. Whistling shell, with long trails of phosphorescent fire, crossing the curves of others, descending to explode with meteoric splendor, made the dark vault above the background of a picture which no painter's skill could transfer to canvas and no language can describe. The hills and plains around the devoted city, its streets and paved sidewalks, its largest buildings of brick or stone trembled in the mighty concussion as though in the throes of some volcanic eruption; flames from burning gunboats on the river and from houses in the city would shoot their forked tongues high above the clouds of sulphurous smoke, the lurid footlights of a stage on which had been set a drama grandly tragic in its every feature.

After the passage of the gunboats by our batteries above mentioned, the defense of Vicksburg assumed entirely another character. The enemy could now operate from below and was not tardy in his movements, making a demonstration on our left flank and a naval attack on our works at Haine's Bluff, on the Yazoo, General Grant crossed the Mississippi river near Port Gibson. Every effort was made to hold him in check, but without success. With ever-increasing re-enforcements he continued to advance apparently towards Jackson, but with his eye ever set upon Vicksburg, the prize for which he had been long contending. General Pemberton moved out his army from their entrenchments and offered battle on Baker's Creek, near Raymond, about twenty miles east of Vicksburg, and here, on the 15th of May, was fought one of the bloodiest battles of the war. Our army did not number over 20,000 effective men of all arms, while the enemy opposed to us had actually engaged, according to official reports, over 40,000, and were constantly receiving re-enforcement. Overwhelmed by these largely superior numbers, our army was forced to retreat, losing many, killed, wounded and taken prisoners by the enemy. General Pemberton fell back to his entrenchments on the Big Black River, where he was closely followed by the victorious army of Grant and forced to renew the battle of the 15th. The defense of this entrenched line was but poorly made, and in considerable disorder our demoralized and routed army sought shelter behind the fortifications of Vicksburg. Our only hope now was in receiving reinforcements, which we were informed were on the way to our relief under the command of General Joseph E. Johnston. These never reached us. While General Grant was engaging us at Baker's Creek he sent a large force, under the command of General Sherman, to meet General Johnston's small army and defeat or destroy it. This Sherman did near Jackson, Mississippi, and after completely destroying the railroad, our only way of communication with the east, devastating the country and burning such commissary stores as he could not use, he returned to add his legions to the large army now completely investing the doomed city. Vicksburg was not provisioned for a siege of indefinite extent; it was not through either carelessness or wilful neglect. General Pemberton has been severely censured for this seeming neglect as he had been in command of this department for at least six months prior to the advance of General Grant, and had fortified Vicksburg, evidently in anticipation of a siege.

We were now completely invested, cut off from all communication with the outside world, destined to endure the sufferings of hunger, disease and every privation of a besieged garrison. Our enemy soon constructed batteries and opened a fire from heavy guns on the devoted city. Heretofore the bombardment was from the gunboats on the river front, but now came a rain of shell from all directions. It was at this time that those of the citizens who had not made their escape were forced to find safety in subterranean abodes where women and children would spend the long, weary days of the siege in the pitiless heat of June. Before the advance of the invading army from the Big Black region, many of these good people were encamped in the woods, near the city, where they were merry as if on a marooning party.

It would be a severe tax upon the patience of the reader were I to give the details of my humdrum life during the forty-eight days of the siege of Vicksburg. In a few days after it had fairly commenced our rations of food, poor at best, were reduced one-third, shortly after one-half, and not long after to almost nothing. I have often seen the poor, half-famished mules and horses slaughtered to furnish the hungry men with meat, and was glad to get a small steak to keep company with my bread, made of cowpeas, ground into a mealy substance, and now and then a wharf rat as a side dish. Our only excitement was in meeting the repeated assaults of the enemy which, even with our small and constantly decreasing numbers, we would invariably repulse.

The division commanded by General Loring had been cut off from our main body at Baker's Creek, reducing our army to such a small number that to man our works we were in single line, the men standing at intervals of three feet or more. Yet so steady was our aim, so cool and deliberate these men, that not a single assault on our works was in the least successful. On the river front had been mounted a very superior Whitworth rifle gun, the whistling noise of its shell readily suggesting the name by which it was known to our men and registered in the history of these eventful days. "Whistling Dick" would occasionally inform us that some naval officer was reckless enough to try and pass our guard, and so with "Long Tom," a thirty-pound Parrot, mounted in an adjoining battery. When these guns were fired we knew that there was some fun, generally connected with a tragedy, giving diversion from the weary monotony of the trenches. Flanking a large transport with cotton bales piled high above her gunwales, a dark night would be selected on which, under a high-steam pressure, the vessel would make the venture, sometimes under the escort of one or more gunboats. It was very rare that either transport or gunboat passed the gauntlet of our batteries or the accurate fire of "Whistling Dick." A well-directed shell or hot-shot would ignite the cotton bales, soon enveloping the transport in a sheet of flame that would light the dark shores and water of the Mississippi River for miles around. Thus I have witnessed the destruction of more than one of these large vessels, and have seen at least one fine gunboat go down under the fire of our well-served artillery.

Picket duty, which was the dread of a soldier in open field, now became a release from the dull sameness and oppressive heat, the discomfort, if not real suffering, of service in the trenches. It gave us some excitement, and while more or less attended with danger, was at least a temporary release from our monotonous garrison duty. When in the trenches there was no possible way to protect one's self from the blistering rays of a tropical sun, our only shelter being under a blanket, stretched over a frame of sticks, and here we would remain day after day, constantly under the fire of the besieging enemy, cooking our mule meat and pea bread as best we could amid a swarm of mosquitoes, with water taken from shallow wells and springs of the bayous. That was a fruitful source of typhoid, dysenteries and malarial poison. Such was the effect of this diet and exposure that at the surrender of our army, at least one-fourth of the men yet alive were in the hospitals, leaving but comparatively a corporal's guard to man the works. Yet throughout the ordeal I never heard a murmur of complaint. We were in the service of our beloved country, inspired by patriotic devotion, and fighting for what we sincerely believed to be just and right. Our privations, and at times real suffering, provoked many a witty remark and laughable joke. At one moment a comrade would be heard cursing the mosquitoes and in the next cheering for Jeff Davis and the cause of Dixie.

So the long, long, weary days passed. With our ranks constantly depleted by disease and death, and the mule meat, rats and pea bread nearly, if not quite consumed; assured that the siege could not be raised by a long hoped-for army of relief, there was but one of two alternatives left for our general commanding: either to evacuate Vicksburg or to surrender his starving army. To consider which of these alternatives he had best adopt, General Pemberton called a council of war on the morning of the 3d of

July. It was found impossible to withdraw the army and preserve its moral. So closely connected were the besieging forces and so strongly guarded every way of egress, that, had the attempt been made to force a passage through the enemy's lines, our army would have been captured or cut to pieces. A majority of the council were of the opinion that it was physically impossible to cut through the enemy's lines and carry the works obstructing the exit, works known to be as formidable as our own. The minority, among whom was the lieutenant-general commanding, were of a contrary opinion and advocated an effort to cut our way out. The position taken by the majority of the conferring generals was, under the circumstances, in my opinion, after being made aware of our true condition, not only sensible, but such as did not compromise the honor of either the commanding general or his devoted army. In addition to the fact that our provisions were exhausted, it was known to our generals if concealed from the men, that our principal defensive works were undermined and that more than one sap had been advanced to the center of our strongest forts. Furthermore, it was sensibly argued that should our works be carried by assault, which now appeared very probable, no terms could be expected and all the horrors of a sacked city were to be anticipated and if possible avoided.

Two or three days before the surrender occurred, it was rumored among our men that our forts were to be blown up by the enemy on the 4th of

July, and a grand assault was to follow in celebration of the anniversary of national independence. Then, for the first time, we became aware of what afterwards was a demonstrated fact, that we were living above magazines in which tons of powder were ready for a match to send us sky-high into Eternity. The opinions of the majority of his generals prevailing, General Pemberton yielded to their discretion and at once opened negotiations with General Grant for terms of capitulation. After the surrender General Pemberton remained with his army attending, as best he could, to their wants and sharing with them the hardships of a march to Enterprise, Mississippi, where the Army of Vicksburg was dissolved on parole. It is not within the scope of this reminiscence to make a vindication of General Pemberton from the harsh criticisms made by some on the administration of his department, and especially against the aspersions of those who have sought to defame his character by alleging a conspiracy or agreement with General Grant, that he should surrender his army on the fourth of July, the great festival day of the United States. Such is the unfortunate fate of those who meet with adversities, that often they are made the scapegoats of others, who seek to lay the blame for their own derelictions upon the innocent and the blameless. As well might it be charged against the incorruptible Lee, that he had fixed upon the fourth of July for the defeat of his army at Gettysburg.

The march of eighty-five miles from Vicksburg to Enterprise was one uninterrupted tramp over dusty roads, through the heat of a July sun and amid the desolate ruins of a country devastated by the raids and the occupation of the Federal armies. The majority of our men were scarcely able to stand. Wasted by disease, poisoned by the malaria of Mississippi swamps, half starved, dejected in spirits, there was but one single inspiring thought, one only hope to nerve our exhausted bodies and stimulate us to exertion – we were on our way home. Home, Sweet, Sweet Home! How I had sighed for its comforts and longed for the shelter of its protecting roof. On this dreary march, and at a cheerless bivouac, I found my mind wandering over the scenes and playgrounds of my happy childhood. In my dreams the old homestead stood vividly before me, and at its portals I could see my waiting father's form as he stood ready to welcome the return of his long absent boy. Who can understand, what philosophy can explain the wonderful, mysterious telepathy of the human mind?

After many provoking delays, I reached the railway depot at Adairsville, Ga., one mile and a half from our home in the country. There I found an elder brother waiting to meet me. He had but a short time before returned home to recover from a wound received in battle. His presence at the depot was indeed a most gratifying surprise to me, the first knowledge I had of his return from the army in Virginia. We were soon at home; a realization so graciously delightful as almost to overcome me with indescribable emotions. My dear old father was standing in the front portico just as I had seen him in my dreams, more than ready, with opened arms to welcome me home. On all sides the servants came to add to our rejoicing, while even the dogs that had followed me on many a hunt through our woods and fields, plainly evidenced their recognition of an old friend. The "fatted calf" was soon killed, and for a time the suspense of anxiety gave place to the realization of long deferred hopes. Bathing in the limpid waters of a near-by stream, clean clothes, and a generous diet, soon restored me to health, while the presence of loved ones and ever-calling neighbors renewed the spirits of my younger days. With my brother I soon found myself the center of attraction for those of the older men and boys of the neighborhood whose age exempting them from field service, did not by any means lessen their interest in the success of our country's cause. One from Virginia and the other from the western army could, in their war experiences and observations, give to many an hour's entertainment; a soldier's story of the march, the bivouac, and of the battles' grim and ghastly glory.

Thus went by the pleasant hours and ever shortening days of the late summer months and early fall. Content to remain at home, surrounded by those we loved, and whose sympathies were the reciprocal relations of congenial friendships, we might have been, were we deaf to our country's call and insensible to the obligations of duty. Thoroughly restored to health, my brother agreed with me that we should return to service in the army and again risk the rage of battle under the colors we had heretofore followed, but in a different line of service. We had obtained sufficient experiences as infantry soldiers and determined to provide ourselves with good mounts in the ranks of some cavalry regiment. We selected the Sixth Georgia, then commanded by Colonel Hart and on duty in East Tennessee, in which command were some of our acquaintances. Again, with almost tearful good-byes, we were off to the war and soon on our way, far from the loved ones at home. We had not joined the so-called cavalry of the western army long before we found out that a release from hard service and much exposure was only the imagination of a broken-down foot soldier. I did not know how they were drilled and maneuvered under Stewart and Hampton in Virginia, but certainly the command we had now joined in Tennessee was at best no more than mounted infantry. I doubt if the officers of the regiment, who were from the walks of civil life, knew the difference between a fierce point and a right or left moulinier. Yet these were brave, chivalrous men, ready always to dare, and, if necessary, to die in the discharge of duty. As mounted infantry their movements were more rapid than if on foot, and hence they could strike the enemy when least expected and retire if opposed by a superior force to make another attack on his flanks or rear. As auxiliaries these mounted regiments proved to be indispensable rendering much effective service. I had heard the statement often made that a dead soldier with spurs on his boots was never to be seen, but soon found out that this was but the idle fancy of some jealous infantryman and as to the easy place I had been seeking for, surely there was no easy place to be found in the ranks of the gallant Sixth when at the front.

The winter of 1863-4 was one of the severest we had known for years, I think, by far the severest I had ever experienced. Poorly clad, with several men without shoes, the earth covered most of the time with deep snows, there was real suffering among the men in the mountains and bleak winds of East Tennessee. Yet these men, who were supposed to be having "a good time," stood manfully to the post of duty, suffered and endured without the murmur of complaint through the most trying ordeals, and were often found dead on the field of battle with spurs strapped to their boots. I was now again in an enemy's country, with "hogbacks" and "bushwhackers" on every hand, the crack of whose rifles coming form some mountain crag was often the death knell of some unwary Confederate. These people had acquired the lurking ways of Indians and in their methods of war were fully the equals, if not superior to the red savages, among whom their ancestors lived and from whom they had acquired their crafty, cunning and cruel instincts. Perfectly familiar with every mountain trail, every highway and byway of the country, they would often sneak at night to the rear of some exposed picket, whose mutilated body would be found the next morning, where the poor fellow had been murdered and left to attest their savage brutality.

On one occasion a "hogback" citizen who had visited our camp ostensibly to sell eggs and chickens to the men, discovered the location of an important picket post where we had a detachment on duty. A night or two after he had been making his protestations of friendship while driving a good bargain with the unsuspecting Confederates, this "hogback" piloted a large force of the enemy to the rear of the picket camp which was soon surrounded and completely cut off from the main body of our regiment. Without a challenge or a demand of surrender the cowardly brutes fired upon the picket, killing some, wounding others and taking off the remainder to suffer a worse fate. Having his enemy completely cut off from support, and at his mercy, a brave foe, governed by the rules of civilized war, would have at least made a demand to surrender before opening fire on those found off their guard, but the Federal troops and their allies in East Tennessee were not fighting that way.

A ruthless war of rapine and murder was waged with unrelenting vindictiveness against those citizens who in any manner expressed a sympathy for the Confederate cause. These were forced to leave their homes and find refuge in Georgia or in more civilized sections of their native State, where some have remained to this day useful and excellent citizens.

During the month of January 1864, our regiment broke camp and marched towards Sevierville, Tennessee, crossing the beautiful Frenchbroad River at Newport. About six miles from Sevierville, we were drawn up in line of battle, near MacNutt's mill, and here had a spirited engagement with the enemy. In this battle I was severely wounded, a misfortune which caused my capture and subsequent imprisonment, thus ending any further active service in the field on my part. I had been engaged in thirteen hard contested battles, had endured the privations incident to the siege of Vicksburg; was with the besieging force at Cumberland Gap and now, when least expecting it, received in comparatively an insignificant engagement a wound which came near ending my life. The fates had decreed that I was yet to endure greater suffering, more privations, and to fill to its overflowing my soldier's cup of bitter experiences in the wretched surroundings of a Yankee prison pen at Camp Chase, Ohio.

An early monument to the
Confederate dead at Camp Chase.

CHAPTER TWO

☆ ☆ ☆ ☆

Wounded and a Prisoner of War

On the 27th of January near Seviersville, Tennessee, I received in battle a wound in my face and neck which at the time was thought to be mortal. The enemy's bullet entering at the symphysis of the chin, shattered my lower jaw bone and passing through the neck made its exit a little to the left of the vertebral column. At the time I received this wound I was on horseback, but soon fell to the ground, bleeding profusely and partially paralyzed. I can recall but slightly the sensation at first experienced when reeling in the saddle. I fell forward, clutching at the neck of my horse, to which I endeavored to cling, and from which I fell senseless to the ground. I have a distant recollection of trying to free my feet from the stirrups and of my apparent inability to move them. Like my arms, the lower extremities had felt the paralysis that left my body entirely only after months of great physical pain. When I regained consciousness I found Yankee soldiers standing around me while their army was passing by, and discovered that I had been rifled by these remorseless thieves from head to foot, each straggler as he came up, turning my limp body over in search of some trophy that might have been left by the preceding thief, At last the "good Samaritan" came in the person of one who, while he wore the uniform of an enemy, had within him the impulses of an honest Christian heart. Approaching me he gently asked if I wanted a drink of water. It was impossible for me to speak but I answered the good man by nodding my head affirmatively, when he at once handed me his canteen. I managed with great difficulty to swallow a little, as my throat was constantly filling with blood and its muscles partially paralyzed. My friend then asked me if I wanted a surgeon. Understanding from my signs that I would be glad to have some medical attention, he went off and soon returned with a surgeon who, without ceremony and very roughly, examined the wound but neither checked the hemorrhage nor gave me any relief from the agonizing pain of my broken jawbone, which I have since learned that he might easily have done. As an excuse for his indifference, the surgeon said that he had the wounded of his army to look after, and to a bystander roughly declared, that I would die anyhow and that it was useless to lose time when he was much needed elsewhere on the battlefield. With a great effort I asked him for pity sake to stop the hemorrhage and give me a chance to live, but with heartless indifference he turned away and left me to die on the frozen ground of this bleak and dreary region.

Under the direction of an impulse, I cannot account for, (as I was not then versed in surgical anatomy) I grasped my throat below the fractured jaw and, pressing upward, found the hemorrhage to cease; as soon as I would release my hand from this feeble grasp, below the fractured jaw, the flow of blood would commence again to fill my throat and mouth, and thus unwittingly I became my own surgeon. Continuing this compression of the small bleeding arteries there was soon formed a coagulum of blood that, acting as a tampon, finally stopped the flow of blood and saved my life.

Keep in mind, indulgent reader, that the weather was intensely cold, the ground hard frozen with a biting wind. and ever falling snow to add to the arctic conditions that surrounded me, and that exposed to it all, my body depleted by a flow of blood that had dyed my clothing crimson, I was compelled by a partial paralysis to remain uncovered for over five hours, and you may have some conception of my suffering. Our small force had been advancing and retreating before largely superior numbers from early dawn of this, to me, ever memorable day. On the retreat, just before I was wounded, I remembered that we had passed a house a short distance from where I was lying. Night was now fast coming to envelope me in the gloom of its sable mantle. Chilled to the bones of my body, I began to realize the certainty of freezing to death if I remained where I was. Exerting to its utmost my remaining strength, I succeeded in rising first to a sitting position from which I could survey my surroundings, and afterwards staggering to an erect position, I found that the Yankee column had passed and that my only companion was a dead Confederate comrade, whose lifeless body was lying on the opposite side of a large log that had previously separate him from my view. My broken jaw bone was giving me agonizing pain, and in addition the intense cold had brought to my hands and feet the peculiar pangs preceding the numbness of death. With all the will power I could command, holding my jaw in position as best I could, I exerted my utmost strength in an endeavor to reach the house I had seen during the retreat of the morning. I had not moved fifty yards on this agonizing walk when I came upon two stragglers from the Yankee army, who with coarse epithets demanded to know where I was going. Notwithstanding, it was plainly apparent that I was badly wounded, my blood stained clothes and bleeding face and neck evidencing this fact, these heartless "hogbacks" kept me in the road some time, gloating over my helpless condition and with foul oaths denouncing me and the Confederate cause so violently that I expected every moment that with the instincts of savage natures they would end my sufferings then and there with a stab or a bullet from a rifle. Finally one of the two, pointing to a clump of trees on a near by hillside said, in a gruff manner, "there is a cabin up there," and left without offering to assist me to climb over the rocks of this steep hill. By the light of a young moon I made out to slowly climb the ascent, and to reach the log cabin, utterly exhausted and in such pain that no pen can describe.

I found a woman to be the only occupant of the cabin, and a fire burning in uncertain glow, to which, with this good woman's aid, I crawled gratefully for realizing again a sensation of warmth. This good woman with the characteristic sympathy of her sex brought a pillow for my head and aided me to stretch my benumbed limbs on the hearth, a kindness I shall always remember and be grateful for – God bless the good women! Had she driven me from her humble cabin home, I am convinced that the sunlight of another morning would have rested upon my body frozen stiff in death. About nine o'clock, just as I was getting well thawed and beginning to find some release from the pain that had racked my nerves, a wagon drove up to the cabin, and the ruffians I had met in the road entered. I was ordered at once to get up, and while making the effort was seized by these men and almost dragged to the wagon. I had clung with desperation to my pillow given me by the kind woman who had received me under the shelter of her roof and which was now stained with blood from my still bleeding wound, but one of the ruffians ordered me to drop it. My good angel intervened, and at her entreaty I was permitted by the brute to keep it. It proved to be a great comfort to me in subsequent days of suffering.

Without the slightest regard for my suffering,

the wagon into which I had been almost thrown was driven with reckless speed over a very rough road to Sevierville and to the county courthouse, in which had been improved a kind of field hospital for both Yankee and Confederate soldiers. The floor of the courtroom had been covered with wheat-straw, while on the hearth of two small fireplaces a few embers were still burning when I entered this revolting place. I was assisted by the guard to a pile of straw, but as I was very cold and sore from the long, rough ride, I preferred to get as close to one of these small fires where in misery I spent the night. In the meantime nothing had been done towards dressing my wound or alleviating my sufferings. During the morning of the next day an elderly lady came to the courthouse, a real Dorcas on a mission of mercy, looking for the distressed and desiring to minister to their wants. She appeared to be much impressed by my pitiable condition, and with motherly kindness offered the first words of sympathy I had heard since I left the other good woman at her cabin door the night before. Hearing my moans she came to where I was still sitting near the fire-place and gently asked if she could do anything for me. I could only answer by a look which was readily interpreted. My jaw and whole face was so swollen that it was impossible for me to articulate or to open my mouth. Leaving me she soon returned with a cup of nice beef soup, whose fragrance, though tempting, I could not enjoy, as I was still holding the broken bane of my jaw in position and could not swallow without the greatest pain. I expressed my thanks to the good lady by a look of gratitude when she placed the cup of soup on the mantle of the fire-place and left me, to minister to some other unfortunate.

Near midday I was assisted down stairs and ushered into the presence of two physicians. Administering an opiate, my broken bone was set in position, the wound in my neck was dressed and I was taken again up-stairs to a pallet of straw. Under the influence of the opiate administered by the physicians I had fallen asleep and resting quietly when a guard rudely shook me saying, "Come, get up Reb, you have to get away from here," Without further ceremony I was led to an ambulance, which I found waiting in the village street, and almost lifted into it. I had not forgotten my pillow, the valued gift of a true woman; in fact it was all I had to claim as my own. The thieves who found me "wounded and by the wayside," had robbed me of everything, leaving scarce enough to hide my naked body. Blood stained, soiled and in odor offensive, I clung to this pillow, not alone because it gave me some ease from racking pain, but as a memento of a good woman's kindness, I valued it beyond gold or the personal comfort it had given to me.

I had scarcely become seated in the ambulance when an order was given to the driver to "go ahead!" I knew not then where to. As fast as the team of horses could go, they were urged on over a rough road jolting my body up and down and with lurching movements to the right and left, tossing me about as if my body was a mere foot ball. A short distance out from the courthouse hospital I ascertained from the driver that his destination was Knoxville, Tennessee, fifty miles west of Sevierville. Will I ever forget that ride, over a rough mountain road, up hill and down hill, over rocks, ruts and roots, day and night for neat forty hours? It would have been a severe trial for a strong man in perfect health; to one in my enfeebled condition, enduring the torture of a fractured bone with a wound passing entirely through the neck, it was not less than the torture of the rack. The driver of the ambulance appeared to be touched with a feeling of sympathy for me, and did what he could to alleviate my suffering. I regret that I cannot recall his name, as he was quite an exception to the class of ruffians who had been my guards and tormentors and who disgraced the uniform of Federal soldiers.

Arriving at Knoxville, I was quite exhausted, so much so that a guard was deemed unnecessary to secure my person. Indeed I could not have made an escape had I been set at liberty to make the effort. From the ambulance I was carried into a hospital whose inmates I found to be a mixture of Confederate and Federal soldiers, wounded and sick, waiting, like myself the issue of a problematic future. My wounds had to be dressed twice during the morning and evening, which brought to my cot a nurse who was quite rough in the discharge of his duty. A feted pus was now being copiously discharged from both orifices of my wound, threatening to poison what little blood remained in my body, and bringing me down to a low state of emaciation. During the month of March I was transferred to the Female Academy building, which was then known as the "Rebel" Hospital. Here I found none but my unfortunate Confederate comrades who, like myself, had been wounded in battle following the glorious ensign of "Dixie." It is said that "misery loves company," but my misery did not love the company of degraded Federal soldiers whose only past-time was cursing the Rebels and denouncing the cause near to my heart. It was good medicine to get away from them and find myself surrounded by comrades who could share in my woes and reciprocate my sympathies.

With this change of surroundings my general health began to improve. When the milder weather of April came, I had so much improved that with other comrades I was sent to add the experiences of a Yankee prison at Camp Chase, Ohio, to those I had already acquired in the service of the Confederacy. Under escort of a guard, we were marched to the railway cars and were soon on the way to Loudon, Tennessee on the Tennessee river, where we were transferred to a steamboat to be transported to Chattanooga. Our guard on the boat numbered about twenty men under command of a Yankee captain, who, believing that we were sufficiently secure in the saloon of the boat, was apparently very careless in the distribution of his small detail for guard duty. We had been under way but a short time when it was whispered from man to man among the prisoners, that we could and should capture the boat and our negligent guard. Our plan was to wait until night fall, and then rush upon the guard, disarm them and land the boat as soon thereafter as possible. This undertaking was very feasible and had we acted promptly would have been successful. Unfortunately it was thought best by a majority to defer action until a late hour of the night. Alas! when we reached Kingston, some twenty miles from Loudon, a regiment of negro soldiers came aboard at once rendering all chance for the execution of our purpose impossible. At once from elation at the prospect of liberation, we were thrown into the gloom of abject dejection greatly increased by the insolence of the negro soldiers, who with insulting injunctions were not slow in letting us know that they were now our masters. Reaching Chattanooga the next day, we had a foretaste of what we were to experience hereafter by being confined in a filthy jail where a wretched night was spent bewailing our own folly in not having captured the steamboat when we had a chance to do so.

From Chattanooga, we were carried to Louisville, Kentucky via Nashville, at which place we were again confined for a night like convicted fellows in the State Penitentiary.

At Louisville we realized that we were among friends and found much sympathy from the women of this elegant city, famous the world over for its hospitality. The ladies of Louisville who came to our aid did not hesitate to express their admiration for Confederate soldiers, with well filled baskets of provisions and cheering words, their bright smiles of approval gave an especial zest to the feast of good things provided for us by their willing hands. I shall always recall with pleasure and with a sense of gratitude my short stay of two days in Louisville while on the way to a prison pen at Camp Chase. From Louisville we were carried by rail via Jeffersonville, Indiana and Cincinnati to our ultimate destination – Columbus and Camp Chase, Ohio.

While waiting in Cincinnati for the cars to take us on our gloomy journey, we were surrounded by a rabble of men, women and children who with jeer and gibe would insult us in every possible way that their filthy language would permit. "Look at the dirty, ragged Rebels" we could hear on all sides. Yes, we were dirty, ragged and we were Rebels and, moreover, we were proud of our rags, and gloried in being known as Rebels. Rebels against a government of partisans who had outraged the Constitution and defied the laws of God and man in seeking to advance their own interests at our expense. Rebels who had helped to make the name of Confederate Soldier the synonym for chivalric courage, and who in death desired no better epitaph than to have inscribed on their tombstones, "A true, faithful Confederate Soldier."

The crude barracks at Camp Chase.

CHAPTER THREE

☆ ☆ ☆ ☆

Camp Chase, Ohio

It was in the month of April, 1864, weary with a long and uncomfortable travel, suffering from my unhealed wound, chilled by the bleak winds of a climate to which I was a stranger, that with other comrades, I reached the city of Columbus, Ohio, a prisoner of war. We had but a glimpse of this, the capital city of a great State, as we were hurried through its streets to the prison, that for months to come was to be our cheerless, inhospitable and wretched abode. Only those who have had such experience can form an idea of how expectation is excited, as from one temporary place of confinement to another a prisoner reaches the place where he is to suffer, endure or to die. We had heard of these cheerless Northern prisons, of the inhuman treatment of the helpless inmates, and had tried hard to prepare our minds for the realization of a life which had speedily ended in the death of hundreds who had preceded us.

The distance from the city to the prison was but short, but short as it was, I lived a life time of anticipation as we trudged over the frozen ground to the certain doom which an inexorable fate had decreed for me. The hour of our arrival was just before the dawn of day.

In the dim light that flickering lamps gave, there stood before us the long high fencing of a stockade, near the top of which the gleam of steel could be seen as the sentinels paced their beats. Without ceremony we were marched into this enclosure and upon the bare ground, without a fire to thaw our almost frozen fingers, we were left to take care of ourselves as best as we could until the light of another day should reveal to us our cheerless surroundings and introduce us to those who were to be our heartless keepers, and to the many comrades who had preceded us to this terrestrial inferno.

Having been captured in battle, we were but poorly clad, as were all Confederate soldiers at this period of the war, without blankets or over-coats, and in this almost summer garb were ushered into the presence of the first crowned king of a bleak and chilling climate.

The light of a new day had come, and with its coming the old prisoners, who were awakened from their slumbers of the night, seeing us walking over the prison grounds began to exclaim “Fresh fish.” The refrain came back from many others who, aroused by the cry, were coming from their bunks in the prison pews, anxious to see the “Fresh fish.” Very naturally we looked about to see some monger who was bringing in "fresh fish" for our breakfast and began to feel our appetites sharpened in anticipation of a feast after our long fasting. We were soon undeceived, as we discovered that we were the "fresh fish" who were being welcomed to the prison life our predecessors had so long endured. Near midday we were "assigned to quarters" in a small house or shanty whose dimensions were not over 16 by 20 feet.

Twelve men were to occupy this room, for whose sleeping comfort bunks were arranged on each side, one above the other, about two feet apart. Some of the prisoners had blankets and a change of clothing, while others had none. There was a pretense of furnishing these necessary comforts, but if a prisoner had anything having even the semblance of a covering he received no consideration whatever. As far as clothing, bedding, shoes, and other necessities of wearing apparel were concerned, we managed to get through the summer months without actual suffering, but when the chilling winds, the frost and ice of this bleak region came, with our bodies wasted by starvation, without fires sufficient to warm our emaciated forms, there came a season of real suffering, of real pain, that ended only in the death of many a helpless victim. To add to our misery, the prison pens were infested with parasites, the miserable tormentors which filth and unjustifiable neglect produced in swarms and which no precaution of ours could possibly prevent, with no means at our command.

My wound had been so long neglected and so poorly healed, that up to the early fall it had not healed, but was continually discharging an offensive pus. It was never dressed, only when some kind comrade would aid me to remove the bandages and wash the wounds with such antiseptics as we could improvise from water and soap. Hence, from bad to worse my general health was on a constant decline, made worse by a deficiency of such common prison food as was in skimpy measure doled out once or twice a day to the half famished victims of the prison commissary.

While we were in the prison hospital at Knoxville, Tennessee, we thought our general treatment was almost inhuman, but after an experience of a few days at Camp Chase, we considered the prison at Knoxville a paradise when compared to our wretched surroundings. This starvation plan, of course, brought about the results which our barbarous enemies desired. The constitutions of the helpless prisoners, however robust, were soon broken down.

Poorly nourished, the body soon became the prey of disease, and death waited at a high carnival of mean and cowardly vindictiveness. Often have I drawn the coarse and unwholesome ration, issued for a whole day of twenty-four hours, and devoured it at one meal without giving relief to my ever present hunger, and have seen many others do the same. Every soft bone and gristle of the spoiled beef was ravenously eaten, and the harder bones treasured to be broken and boiled, whenever we could do so, in hope that we could get a taste of the marrow or grease that might be left upon them. Time and again, the guards would order away these starving men from the garbage wagon and swill tubs, where they were eagerly hunting for a crumb of bread or a bone that a well fed dog would have refused.

These scenes and unexaggerated details of a Yankee prison have been most graphically portrayed by Dr. John A. Wyath, in an article contributed to the *Century Magazine* for April 1891. My experiences at Camp Chase corroborate all that he has written of the administration at Camp Morton. It was undoubtedly the policy and the studied plan at both places to "starve the Rebels into the submission of death."

Men who had proven themselves to be such in the ordeal of battle, who at their homes were the best of citizens, and in the army respected for their honesty and soldierly conduct, had become so demoralized by the pangs of hunger that they would feed like hogs upon the refuse thrown into the swill tubs from the hospital and mess hall kitchens.

When we first entered the prison we were allowed to purchase certain articles of food from the prison sutler. There was some understanding between these thrifty Yankees and the infamous superintendent of the prison, by which tickets were to be issued to the prisoner – each ticket representing a certain money value and forthwith our money was all taken from us, and in exchange we were furnished with the superintendent's tickets. This meant, of course, that we should only purchase from the sutler, and that we would have to pay several hundred per cent more for what we did get than the same thing could have been bought for with cash elsewhere. It was nothing more or less than robbery, the mean stealing of the superintendent and his sutler from the helpless prisoners.

There were but few among us fortunate enough to have money or who could be supplied with it by friends outside. For a time these fared very well, but it was not long before the sutler's store was closed, and the victims left with the unredeemed tickets of the rascally superintendent. Every means was used to prevent our friends outside or at our homes from knowing our real condition. No letter was allowed to leave the prison that was not read and censored by the superintendent, and his postmaster.

If anything was written that reflected upon the management, if any complaint was made or appeal sent to our friends for relief, the letter went into the waste basket. From the day the sutler's store was closed, the death-head and skeleton fingers of starvation appeared in Camp Chase. Scant as our rations were, they were reduced and no salt issued. Our only means of obtaining salt was by boiling down the brine in the empty and discarded fish kits, which, when obtained, gave out a most offensive odor. It was this, or no salt at all.

Early in the summer of 1864, the prison was crowded by an influx of many unfortunates from the armies of the Confederacy. New houses or shanties were hastily built of rough planks, about eighteen feet wide and eighty feet long with bunks arranged on each side, and hallway through the center about five feet wide. It was without ceiling, and the floor of green lumber, with cracks between the planks wide enough to let the cold wind freely circulate. In mid-summer it would have answered as a lodging place, but in the climate of Camp Chase, was not less than the sure breeding place of pneumonia and other pulmonary affections. At one end of the long shanty was a room used as a kitchen, with a small opening in the partition large enough only for a plate or cup to be passed through. No bucket or pitcher was furnished to keep water in, our only vessel being an ordinary sized tin cup. An order had been issued that no water should be thrown about the pump by those who went there to quench their thirst. One of the unfortunates, not aware of the order, washed out his tin cup at the pump and threw out the water on the ground before filling the cup with water to drink. A guard seeing him throw the water on the ground, at once fired at him and missing his aim severely wounded an unlucky prisoner standing some distance beyond him, breaking his leg, rendering it necessary in the judgment of the Yankee surgeon to amputate the poor fellow's fractured limb. At another time I witnessed the maiming of a prisoner by a guard for the most trivial violation of an order. A ditch had been dug through the center of the enclosure for the purpose of conveying the refuse and detritus of the camp. This ditch was flushed from a large tank at the upper end, which we were required to fill every day by pumping the water, in details. An order was issued requiring all the prisoners to assemble on the south side of the ditch and bring their blankets with them. The superintendent, or prison keeper, took stand at the end of the line near the prison wall, and the men were ordered to recross the ditch near them bringing their blankets. The effect of this, as we ascertained afterwards, was to find out who had more than one blanket. If a prisoner had more than one, he was required to drop the surplus and allowed to retain only a single blanket. One of the prisoners, not understanding the movement, stepped across the ditch before the order to do so was given, and was immediately shot down by the guard. The poor fellow's leg was so badly shattered that amputation was rendered necessary, another one made cripple for life. Of course nothing was done to these cowardly guards. Doubtless they were complimented for gallantry and are now drawing pensions from the United States Treasury, on certificates of meritorious service.

At a certain hour at night, the guards would cry out, "Lights out," and if the lights were not immediately extinguished, the guard would fire into the room regardless of whom he might kill or maim. No friend of a suffering comrade dare make a light, however extreme the illness, or imminent the peril of the sufferer, or to speak above a whisper during the night watches. If so, the bullet from the rifle of a guard would come whistling into the barracks to kill or to wound some luckless sleeper.

Attempts at escape were frequent, and met with the severest punishment. These attempts to escape from this terrible place, were often made and many ingenious plans resorted to, generally without success, and always followed by the most inhuman tortures. In the prison were spies, in the disguise of Confederate soldiers who claimed to have been captured, but who in reality were the tools of our ever vigilant and heartless enemy. Again we had, I am ashamed to admit it, a few who were really at one time Confederates, but who had compromised every principle of honest manhood, by deserting their comrades, and for the pay of good food and an easy time, were ready to give to our keeper information of any plan or combination designed to give us the liberty we so much longed for. These we called "razor backs," the despised agents of a merciless enemy whom we dreaded in their meanness and cowardice, as we would the sneaking presence of an assassin. Subject as we were to the espionage of these "razor backs," and to the watchful vigilance of many guards, knowing full well that a failure to escape meant a suspension by the thumbs until the anguish of pain would drive some into insanity, or ordered to hard labor on the grounds with a ball and chain fastened to one's feet and legs, or to be "bucked and gagged" daily, for hours at a time and left to lie in this wretched condition on the frozen ground; or to be maimed for life by being shot in the legs; yet, with all these tortures witnessed by us daily, in the desperation of suffering and starvation, men would often run the risk of escape. How shall we manage to make our escape from this infernal place, from the nauseating filth and stench of our prison, from the certainty of a lingering death, and the cruelty of our inhuman keepers, formed the burden of our thoughts by day and gave fantasms of vision to our dreams by night.

I have no words at my command with which to describe the horrors of the Yankee prison at Camp Chase. One would have to follow "Dante" in his descent to Hell, and in his wanderings among its inmates, to find an approach to it. Then why not try to remain passive; it could not be more than death to make the effort.

The walls surrounding the prison grounds were very high, twenty feet at least, and well lighted at night. On a platform, near the top, sentinels were pacing to and fro and never out of sight of each other or of the prisoners. Nevertheless, now and then on some dark or stormy night desperate prisoners would make the effort to scale these walls. In a very few instances the attempt was successful, but the majority were either shot or doomed to the torture of thumb cords.

The entrance to the prison was secured by a large and strongly constructed double gate, always guarded by a detachment of twelve men. A number of our comrades determined to charge the guard and force their way out or die in the attempt, reasoning that it was better to die a death from the rifle ball of a guard than to linger in misery and finally die of starvation. These desperate prisoners getting close to the gate, watched for the coming of the superintendent's bread wagon. As soon as the gates were opened, for the wagons to pass in, the gallant prisoners raised the old Rebel yell and rushed out and by the astonished guard. A fusilade of shots immediately announced these escapes, not one of which took effect upon the fleeing prisoners. A detachment of cavalry followed them however, and soon brought back the unfortunate fellows, the worse by far for their gallant charge on the guard of the gate. Poor men! As they came in, it was indeed a sickening sight to see how brutally these poor emaciated creatures had been treated. Their heads and faces bloody with the cuts of sabres and bruises of the brutes who had beaten them with clubs after their capture, until some could scarcely walk. They suffered the severest punishment, and day after day have I had my sympathies taxed for these brave comrades, whose only crime was in seeking to escape the horrors of Camp Chase.

It was about this time that an epidemic of small pox appeared in our midst to add another to the many horrors of our inferno, Fortunately I had been vaccinated, rendering me immune to variola but not to varioloid, a mild form of the loathsome disease. If there could have been a doubt in my mind as to the efficacy of vaccination, it was all removed by my experience. In some form, I, in common with all the prisoners, who had not suffered with the disease before, was a victim. How could it have been otherwise, packed up together as we were in the limited space of a prison enclosure? The atmosphere was loaded with the sickening virus of the disease, and to escape, if at all susceptible, was an impossibility. My mess mate, Reuben Evans, occupying the bunk with me, was stricken down first and soon developed a marked case of confluent small pox. He woke me at midnight and in a whisper informed me that he was very ill with what he believed was the then prevailing disease. I gave the poor fellow water and the next morning and upon examination found him broken out with small pimples and a high fever. Poor fellow, he begged me most piteously to let him remain with me, declaring that he would die if sent to the pest house. Well may he have thought so. Day after day the dead were taken from that charnal house, over whose door might have been written, "he who enters here leaves hope behind." I kept him concealed and said nothing to others of his real condition, well knowing that I could not escape the disease in some form, even though he should be taken from me. I would go to bed with him at night as though nothing was the matter with him, and in every way possible kept his real condition from the knowledge of the prison officials. I kept him well wrapt until the pustules were drying up and he began to convalesce.

Evans recovered, but it was a very "close call." During his convalescence some one of the prisoners reported his case. He was at once taken out, but was returned in a day or two. Just then I was taken ill, and in return for my kindness, Evans stuck to me like a true man, doing all in his power for my relief. To let the physicians know my real condition, was a certain consignment to the hospital, a better name for which would have been the "dead house." Few who entered its horrible walls, ever came out other than in a coffin. Having only the mildest form of the loathsome disease, it was not long before the fever stage passed and I convalesced without the marks or "pits" to disfigure me for life. My rapid convalescence I attribute to the unremitting attention of my mess mate, who in thus returning my kindness to him, was bringing us closer together in the ties of a genuine comradeship.

During the illness of Evans I would draw his skimpy ration for him, and such of it as he did not consume, I ate with ravenous greed. When one considers the utter destitution of the prisoners, the large majority of whom had no change of clothing, the necessity to keep these on the person to hide one's nakedness, or to aid in producing warmth enough to keep one from freezing in the winter; when made aware of the want of any system of hygiene in the prisons, and of the abundant filth which I have in no wise exaggerated, the wonder will be, not that we had epidemics of small pox, but how we escaped every known disease of the body that humanity is heir to.

At one time there was an issue of wheat straw to soften the hard side of the planks upon which we slept. This straw remained in the bunks until the movement of our bodies had ground it into a powder. While this straw helped to keep us warm, and eased the deadening discomfort of a bare plank to our emaciated bodies, it was the breeding place, the very nidus of vermin, that swarmed over our bunks and lodged in every crack and crevice of the prison barracks. The clothing of the prisoners was infested with these disgusting pests who day and night were tormented with their bites. Time and again I have seen these poor fellows beating their shirts over a board to knock them off, and holding their clothing over the flames of burning paper in a vain effort to rid their garments of these ever multiplying pedicules. Even if soap and water could be obtained, washing the clothes was of no avail. As soon as dried the vermin would appear as vigorous and as vicious as ever.

Such is the constitution of our human nature, that, even in the most abject circumstances, surrounded by the despicable attendants of wretched poverty, deprived of all in intellectual employments, and with associations, or environments that would check every lofty impulse of the soul; even in such a condition, a mind not yet sunk into the apathy of idiocy, or wrecked by its contact with loathsome things, would find some diversion, some surcease for its sorrows, some way in which to bring to the famishing soul a single pleasure, however trivial. One can scarcely imagine that there could be any fun, any real amusement in watching the antics of a miserable louse, and certainly less to inspire a poetic thought. Robert Burns might write a poem on the creeping thing he saw on the ribbon of a pretty girl in a Kirk of Scotland, but is it possible that a poor forlorn prisoner in the destitution of the meanest poverty, could get a moment's real fun in playing with the miserable tormentor that had crawled over his back and rendered his life a constant affliction? What think you, gentle reader, of a louse race, of a regular pugilistic encounter between two champions of the genus *pediculidae*. I have witnessed both and have seen many a potato won and lost, by the owners of these tormentors.

The race course, if race it was to be, was on the surface of an inverted tin pan. This would be sufficiently heated to produce a lively movement of the louse without destroying life. Those who were the owners of the coursers had carefully selected the largest and most vigorous pedicules from their large herd and brought them up to the appointed place of meeting where they were exhibited, and formally entered for the race under some name such as Sheridan, Sherman, Pope or Hunter. Our men thought too much of their own chivalrous generals to give their names to a miserable louse, however active the insect might have been. When all was ready, at a given signal the racers would be thrown together in the center of the heated tin, and at once away they would go, making every effort to escape the heat that was warming them up to their work. The goal was the periphery of the pan, the one reaching this circle first to be declared victor in the race. It was noticeable that these insects would invariably run in a constantly extending circle, round and round the center from which they started until the rim or outer edge of the inverted pan had been reached where they would fall off and be recovered by their owner. Surprising though it may be to you, yet I have seen a room full of grown men thrown into great excitement over these races, at which many an unlucky prisoner would lose a day's rations. If it was a fight between two selected lice the same formal arrangements would be made and the same excitement general. The arena was again the tin pan or plate, unheated. Bringing these insects together, only a little encouragement was necessary to excite them into a violent passion and the fight would begin (often continuing for several moments) and only ending on the death or the retreat of one or the other of the combatants.

Virgil looking on such a scene would hardly have exclaimed, *"Dens fecit hace Ohum vobis."* Of course, in such a large and promiscuous crowd there were "many men of many minds." An old and well worn deck of cards in whist, draw poker, and other games, gave entertainment to some. Others had improvised checker boards and chess men, while others of less philosophic spirits would mope and sigh, hugging their sorrows to aching hearts, until notalgia or wasting disease would end their miserable lives in the gloom of death. Now and then, when the weather was favorable, a prison ball would enliven our spirits and give real pleasure to the participants. A number would be selected to represent ladies. These, to distinguish them from the men, would run strings through the center of their blankets and tie these around the waist. As there was no room large enough for the dancers, the ball would be held in the open plaza or street of the prison. Among our comrades were some superior musicians, and many who were graceful and accomplished in the various dances that had often given zest to the life of our Southern people. Partners would be selected for the several dances, and their names entered on slips of paper with all the ceremony of a regular ball. The "floor manager" would announce the dancers, call the figures and direct the whole entertainment just as though he was in a ball room in New Orleans or Richmond. After a grand march the lively cotillion, graceful waltz, and stately lancers, would be followed by an old Virginia reel to the infinite delight of the dancers, and the entertainment of those who were lookers on. Even our Yankee guards appeared to enjoy the occasion and never interfered to break up the merry dance of our gallant comrades.

Some of the over 8,000 Confederate prisoners
held at Camp Chase.

CHAPTER FOUR

☆ ☆ ☆ ☆

Departure From Camp Chase – Stay at
Camp Winder – Return Home

During the month of February 1865, an exchange of prisoners was agreed upon between the Federal and Confederate authorities. To my inexpressible joy, I was among the first division to leave the long detested prison that for three hundred weary days had been my horrible lodging place.

By railway we were moved to Baltimore via Wheeling, Va., and from Baltimore to Aikens Landing on the James River and from that place marched through the picket lines of our enemies, on our way to Richmond, the capital of our beloved land of Dixie.

Can I ever forget the emotions I experienced when I looked upon the grand battle flag and the national colors of the Confederacy, when I was again with my own people and breathing once more the soft air of the land of the pessamine and the gay woodbine? As soon as my comrades realized that they were freed from the presence of the hated Yankee, and were again under the aegis of the flag that symbolized the chivalry of Dixie, a mighty cheering yell of gratitude was given that might have been heard for miles.

I felt a thrill of emotion passing from my heart to the extremities of my body as if some elixir had been given to me from the hand of a gracious God. Yes, I was indeed free from the curses and insults of a brutal guard. It was true, that I saw around me a deserted country, but, oh! it was my homeland, and I was now on the way to my own sweet home, where every love of my soul centered itself.

Yes, again, through the mercy of a kind Providence, I was again in the sunshine of my native land of flowers, the breeding place of noblest women and bravest men. With a more elastic step than I had made for many months, I followed my comrades to the steam boat waiting to convey us up the historic James River to Richmond, the grand, glorious capital of our Confederacy. It was late in the evening when we arrived in this historic city, the dwelling places of the noblest men and women whose history for generations has made the name of Virginian the synonym of all that was chivalrous, noble, generous and true. Early the next morning we were ordered to Camp Winder, in the suburbs, for a short rest to receive our soldier's pay and furloughs. Buoyed up by excitement, incident to our sudden change from cheerless prison at Camp Chase, to the realization of freedom among sympathizing friends, I had managed to keep up with my stronger comrades, but I now found my emaciation from starvation so great that it was impossible for me to walk even a short distance without resting.

During my stay at Camp Winder, I became very ill and came near losing my life by an imprudence, which ill-famished persons are apt to experience. Ten months had passed since I had barely eaten enough to keep me alive, and since I had known an hour when I was entirely free from hunger. Brought now into the presence of food in abundance, I ate more than my stomach could digest. As soon as this was ejected, the pangs of hunger would return, and notwithstanding I well knew what the result would be, I could not refrain from eating more than was proper. The consequence was, that I suffered from a severe attack of acute indigestion. Having received the pay of a Confederate soldier, in the currency of our country, and with a well merited furlough in my pocket, my face was now turned towards the home of my love in North Georgia to meet those from whom I had been long separated by a prisoner's cruel fate. Sherman's force of invading plunderers had swept over the beautiful valley and green hills of my native land, and from the mountains to the seashore had left utter ruin and desolation in their march through the fairest portion of Georgia. My father had abandoned his home upon the approach of the army of invasion and taken refuge near Canton in Cherokee County. There I bent my weary way, and reached his roof in March 1865. There was no mother to welcome me to her bosom, as it had been my irreparable misfortune to lose her gentle admonition and loving caresses in my early youth, but there was somewhere the manly heart of a devoted father whom I well knew was more than ready to greet his soldier boy. When I reached the house I found that my father was absent, having gone to North Carolina on business, but was expected to return shortly. The servants were evidently rejoiced to see me. These people I had known from my infancy as the servants of my father. I had grown into manhood with the children of the older generation, between whom and my father, there was a relation which the theorist of cold-blooded New England never knew or apparently cannot understand.

These old servants were not demoralized at that date by the Freedman's Bureau, but remained the same true friends I had known from my child-hood. They were really glad to see me again, coming among them as one from the dead. Among the first things I asked for was a change of clothing, telling them frankly what my true condition was and asking their aid to rid me of the abominable insects that had been my tormentors in prison and my reminder of its horrible surroundings. My clothes could not be found among the articles brought from our home, but after a while a suit was brought me with a change of underclothing which proved to be that of some one else. Thus provided, I went with one of the servants to a river not far off, and with a plenty of strong soap was soon luxuriating in a bath that was a real tonic;

no Roman ever enjoyed a better one. The servants gathered about me on my return to the house evidently delighted to see "Mass John" home again. My good father returned home in a few days from his visit to Carolina. Before reaching the house someone had informed him that I had returned safe, the first information of my being alive that he had received for many months. He was overcome with emotions I had never seen him evidence before, when he met and embraced his long lost boy. With a trembling voice, and his eyes suffused with tears, he said, "My son! I would never have known you had I not been told that you were here!"

Reader, have you ever experienced a warm loving embrace of a father's love, after a long absence, in which his yearning soul was depressed with doubt or elated with a hope as to whether he would ever meet you again? If not, be assured that it is just such trials, just such experiences that bring human souls nearer together in this life, than any other circumstances can ever bring about. We remained at Canton until April, when my father returned to the old homestead and amidst ruins began again to start life's struggles.

An old photograph of the Confederate prisoners
at Camp Chase, taken over the wall.

CHAPTER FIVE

☆ ☆ ☆ ☆

Radical Reconstruction – Ku Klux Klan –
Tribute to Southern Women

In the preface to these pages I have attempted to describe the condition of our stricken country and the demoralization among our servants incident to the infamous proceedings of the "Freedman's Bureau," a feature of Radical Reconstruction that brought as much material loss to the South, if not much more than the devastating march of the Federal armies and the plundering cohorts that formed their rank and file. I assure the reader that in no particular is this description exaggerated. The mean, vindictive, cowardly spirit of the Yankees who had overpowered us, the Southern soldiers, by superior numbers, was made all fully manifest in the systematic manner in which the so-called Reconstruction measures of the Radical Congress were enforced by the carpet baggers who were sent to feast like Harpies on their helpless victims.

There are many dark chapters in the history of nations, claiming to be civilized and enlightened by the Christian religion, but none can be darker than the infamous record made by these accidental victors who in the name of liberty inaugurated every crime of despotism; who with the hypocritical cant of a Puritanical religion used the commandment of Jehovah to suit their own plundering conveniences, and with a fanatical zeal, unsurpassed by the followers of Mohammet, actually seized the altars of our sacred temples and profaned them by offerings of thanksgiving to a God whose lairs they had openly defied. Yes, the general conduct of the Federal armies, during the War between the States, and the legislation of the Federal Congress, following these uncivilized horrors, will forever remain a blot upon the escutcheon of the United States, and a severe commentary upon Christian civilization. And yet, if a protest was made against these monstrous outrages, if petitions were filed against these barbarous iniquities, a cry of "disloyalty," was raised and citizens of the highest social rank, whose known integrity could not be impeached, were marched to prison by miserable hirelings who were often found in possession of personal belongings they had stolen from their prisoners.

The year eighteen hundred and sixty-five will be ever memorable among the citizens of northwest Georgia, as one of great privation and suffering. The retreat and the advance of two large armies with their ever attendant camp followers, spreading out over an area of many miles, is, under the best of discipline, a scourge to any country. Such was the vindictive spirit of the men who composed the immense invading Federal army, and so absolutely dependent was the Confederate army on the country for supplies that when this terrible scourge of invasion had passed from the once beautiful valley and plain of our section, nothing was left upon which to sustain the helpless women and children. In many instances they were left so destitute and suffered the pangs of hunger to such an extent, that they have been known to visit the camping grounds of the enemy and feed upon the corn and fragments of food left at the bivouacs of the soldiers. It was back to my boyhood home in this devastated section that I had come to wander among scenes that in pathetic somberness were on every hand the mute monuments of human passion. Fortunately, our enemies could not capture and carry off with them our climate and fertile soil. This alone remained with the unconquered spirit and indomitable will of our manhood, untarnished by dishonor. Though very late in the season, with such agricultural implements as could be improvised, and with the broken down, half-famished work horses, left to die by the victorious enemy, we went to work to start life all over again. My health was very poor; indeed for a length of time it appeared that my naturally strong constitution had received such a shock and was so weakened by the fearful sufferings of my prison life, that I would never again recover the strength and elastic spirit of former days. In time I began to recover and with the tender care of home affections and the proper food which I had long been deprived of, health, the greatest blessing of bounteous Heaven, came back to renew my strength and enable me to aid in the work of our farm life.

Unpromising as were our surroundings, and hard as was the conflict with want in our desolate region, yet we should have triumphed over all of these adverse conditions, and soon have realized the quiet and prosperity which peace brings to an industrious people, had the malice of our Northern political enemies left us, undisturbed. In the con-fident expectation that the negro could be made the willing tool of their malice, the Radical Republican Congress began a system of what they were pleased to call "Reconstruction" by enacting the "Civil Rights Bill," intended to secure the enfranchisement of the negro, and the humiliation and utter ruin of his former master. Under the provisions of this Act of Congress, the "Freedman's Bureau" was established with its multitude of branches located in every town, village and hamlet of the prostrate South. The negroes were made to believe that the lands of their former masters were to be confiscated and divided into farms of forty acres, and that the Yankee Government would give each head of a family one of these farms, a mule, farming utensils and one year's supply of provisions.

Monstrous as this confiscation would have been and absurd though it appeared to many, yet there were thousands who believed that it was the purpose of the Radical Republican to carry out the nefarious plan. The poor deluded negro was jubilant in expectation of his fortune, and at once became utterly demoralized as a farm laborer. To enforce his right of citizenship, a garrison of soldiers was stationed at every county seat and prominent towns throughout the Southern States, and there the negroes would flock in confident assurance that "Marse Linkum," would give them titles to their forty-acre farms and send them to it on a government mule. All kinds of complaints and claims were made against the white farmers by their slaves, who would present false claims for a large share of the growing crops, and even going so far as to lay claim to a large interest in the stock and farming utensils. These claims were presented to some "Carpet Bagger" magistrate, who had followed the troops stationed at the town to enforce his decision and who would invariably decide in favor of the negro complainant.

It may be readily conjectured by those at all familiar with the ignorant negro and with the unprincipled adventurers who were thus making him their dupes, that this condition of affairs not only disturbed normal business relations between the employer and his hireling, but brought about the utter demoralization of the negro. To such an extent did this go that the farmer feared to leave his family unprotected, while the female members of his household were in constant dread of the brutes who were roaming over the land of the protected vagrants of the Freedman's Bureau. When I read the indignities, the outrages and material losses that our people sustained under the iniquity of the Reconstruction Acts of the Radical Congress, it is only a wonder that we submitted so long to the tyrannical rule of these oppressors.

Finally forbearance ceased to be a virtue and our people actuated by the spirit of true manhood, threw off the yoke of their oppressors. "Ku Klux Klan" was organized in every county in Georgia, and a few night rides drove the miserable "Carpet Bagger" from our stricken State. This organization was in my opinion the logical sequence of our oppression and tyrannical misgovernment. There was no instance known in which the Ku Klux dealt unjustly with either the adventurer from Yankeeland or his poor dupe, the ignorant negro. It was only upon those who were notoriously mean and oppressive that their ghastly shadows fell. A few of these swinging from the limb of a tree in some conspicuous place gave warning to others that the people of Georgia long outraged by an oppression, which no law of God or honest men would sanction, were determined to maintain their rights of citizenship and their virtues of manhood at every cost.

I cannot dismiss this unpleasant reminiscence without a reference to such of the negroes who were true to their former masters and who were wise enough and honest enough not to have been deluded by the "Carpet Bagger" and "Scallawag" politician ruling among them as agents of the Freedman's Bureau. This class of negroes was generally among the older ones who had their characters formed by a long lifetime association with their masters and their white neighbors. Alas, this class of negroes is now fast passing away. The younger generations have not inherited any of their virtues, but appear to be drifting, year after year, farther and farther away from that simple honesty and industrious devotion to duty which characterized their fathers. These older negroes never asserted nor have they ever desired to assert, any right of social or intellectual equality with the white man. To him they were uniformly polite, respectful and in his service, obedient and tactful. Their best friends were at the old homestead that shadowed their humble cabins, and they knew it. It is not so with the younger generations of negroes. It is from this class that all the acts of brutality that shock the moral sense of civilized society, are constantly coming and appear to increase as the generations are farther removed from the régime that gave civilization to their ancestors.

The ever present inspiration that moved the arms of our men, and gave birth to the highest resolves of patriotism, that like a beacon light led them on to the night of gloom that settled upon our land as a pall of death, came from the heroic devotion, the uncomplaining spirits, the constant love and cheering sympathies of our noble women. The mothers of Greek and Roman heroism never gave expression to nobler virtues than our Southern women evidenced all through the severe ordeals of this period in our social and political history. If their faith and encouragement sustained us on the red field of battle, if as ministering angels in mercy sent, they came to the wards of the hospital and gently soothed our pangs of suffering, if like the mother of the Gracchi, they gave us our shields with the injunction to return them from battle with honor, or be brought back upon them, with a spirit not less admirable, with a gentleness not less divine, with a heroism not less grandly noble, did these women of the South stand by their fathers, their brothers and their sons in a desperate conflict with poverty in a land desolated and in ruins. Planting flowers at the graves of their noble dead, they gave renewed energy and high resolve to the living and unconquered manhood of the South. Let us build monuments to the memory of our dead heroes and tell to generations unborn of their more than Roman chivalry, but somewhere the sky of our Southland is brightest and clearest at some place near the heart of our mother land, let the men of the South erect a monument of white stone to the women who were their inspiration in every noble achievement. Let this shaft rise high into the purest atmosphere, where the first rays of the morning's sun shall be its matin welcome and its last rays an evening's benediction. Let it rest upon a massive granite base, upon which shall be inscribed the veneration of men for the women, worthy of their highest admiration.

To these noble women do I dedicate these

reminiscences of my service as a Confederate soldier. If I have faithfully endured until the end, it is because they have lived and I have felt the influences of their heroic spirits and devoted love. God bless the women.

Dr. J.H. King,
Surgeon,
Soldiers' Home, Atlanta, Ga.

Made in the USA
Middletown, DE
24 December 2022

17198069R00050